This book belongs to:

....

igloo

Published in 2011
by Igloo Books Ltd
Cottage Farm
Sywell
NN6 0BJ
www.igloo-books.com

Copyright © 2007 Igloo Books Ltd

B004 0811

2 4 6 8 10 9 7 5 3 1

ISBN: 978-0-85780-068-8

Printed and manufactured in China

My First Bible Stories

Retold by Nick Ellsworth

Illustrated by
Roger Langton and
Sara Sliwinska

The Old Testament

The New Testament

THE OLD TESTAMENT

In The Beginning

GENESIS 1-2

In the beginning there was God. Then God created Earth. But to begin with, Earth was as dark as night. So God said, "Let there be light!" So He made the Sun. Now there was day to go with night.

Then God made the sky and, underneath the sky, He gathered together huge amounts of water to make the seas.

And in-between the seas He made rocks and mountains and soil. Then He made flowers and forests of trees which could grow in the soil.

Then God made fish that could live in the seas and birds that could fly in the sky and animals that could live on the land.

He then made the first man, whom He called Adam. God thought Adam might be lonely all by himself, so He made the first woman, whom He called Eve.

It had taken God six long days to make everything in the world so, on the seventh day, He rested. He decided from then on, every seventh day should be a day of rest.

And this special day of rest He called the Sabbath.

Adam and Eve

GENESIS 2-3

God gave Adam and Eve a beautiful garden to live in, which He called the Garden of Eden. He filled it with the loveliest flowers and plants. There were rivers Adam and Eve could drink from, and trees bearing the most delicious fruit. It was truly paradise.

In the centre of the garden, God planted a special tree.
"This is the Tree of Knowledge of Good and Evil," He told them.
"Do not eat the fruit that grows on it. If you do, you will die."

Adam and Eve lived happily in the garden for many years and made sure that they never ate the fruit that grew on the special tree.

But, one day, a slimy snake slithered up to Eve and hissed, "You really should taste the apples that grow on the Tree of Knowledge. They really are the most delicious fruit in the garden."

Eve was a little frightened.

"But God said we'd die if we tasted the fruit from that tree," she said.

"You won't die!" mocked the snake. "God said that because He knows if you were to eat the fruit, you would become as wise as He, and He wouldn't want that to happen, would He?"

Eve thought this made sense. So she walked slowly to the Tree of Knowledge, picked off the juiciest, ripest apple she could see and took a big bite out of it. And, when she saw Adam a little later, she shared the fruit with him.

When God realized what they had done, He was angry.
"You have disobeyed me," He said. "You must now leave this beautiful garden. From this day on, you must work hard to grow your own food in the rough and thorny ground that lies beyond here. And when you grow old, you will die."

So Adam and Eve left the Garden of Eden. Their lives became much harder, and they struggled to grow enough to eat in the hot, harsh lands outside the Garden of Eden.

For the rest of their days, they regretted the time when they disobeyed God by eating the fruit that grew on the Tree of Knowledge.

Cain and Abel

GENESIS 4

Adam and Eve had two sons. One was called Cain, the other, Abel. Cain worked in the fields growing crops while his brother Abel looked after the sheep on the hills.

They both grew up loving God and tried to please Him in any way they could.

Once, Cain offered some of his freshly cut crops to God, while Abel
offered Him one of his new-born lambs. God was pleased with Abel's
lamb but did not want Cain's crops, thinking they were not worthy of
Him.

Cain was jealous that God had accepted Abel's offering, but not his
own. One day he suggested to his brother that they should go for
a walk together. While they were out, Cain killed his brother.

When Cain returned home, God asked him where Abel was.

"I don't know," replied Cain. "Am I my brother's keeper?"

But God knew what he had done and said, "Your brother's blood cries out to me from the ground. You will be punished for your evil. You will spend the rest of your life wandering the Earth, and you will find no rest."

"But I will be killed by the first person who sees me," cried Cain.

"You will not," said God. "I will put a mark on you that tells people that if they dare to kill you, I will take seven lives in revenge."

So Cain collected his few belongings and left his home forever.

Noah's Ark

GENESIS 6-9

God was angry. He saw that most people on Earth were not obeying him, so He decided to flood the whole world and drown everyone in it.

But there was one man He decided to save. This man's name was Noah. God knew that Noah was a good man and wanted to save him from the flood.

"You and your family must build a great Ark," God told him. "In it, you will gather together two of every animal on Earth. Do this and you will be saved."

Noah and his family set to work. They cut down the tallest trees and used them to make the frame of the Ark. Then they covered the frame with rough planks of wood and put tar on the inside so that water couldn't get in.

They all worked very hard for many months. Finally, it was finished.

Noah then gathered together two of every single creature on Earth, just as God had told him to do. The animals lined up and slowly began to troop into the Ark. There were so many of them, it took a very long time. Everyone helped to load enough food and water to last them for months. Once Noah and his family had joined the animals on board, Noah shut the huge doors behind them.

Then, the rains began.

It rained for forty days and forty nights. Soon, the whole Earth was covered with water and became one big sea.

For months and months, the Ark tossed around on the sea. Noah peered through the windows every day, hoping to see signs of dry land, but he saw only water.

One day he sent out a raven to look for dry land, but the raven didn't return.

Then he sent out a dove to look for dry land, but the dove didn't return, either.

Noah sent out a second dove. When it returned with an olive leaf in its beak, Noah knew this was a sign that the waters were going down, and dry land wasn't too far away.

He sent out the dove once more and this time it didn't return. Noah now knew beyond doubt that the flood had almost disappeared. He looked out of a window and was overjoyed to see dry land on the horizon.

Gathering his family together, Noah told them the news they had waited so long to hear. Then they sailed happily towards the shore.

After he had made sure all the animals left the Ark safely, Noah got down on one knee and thanked God for keeping his family safe.

"I promise," said God, "however angry I become, I will never again destroy what I have created."

Then He put a beautiful rainbow in the sky.
"Whenever I see a rainbow," said God, "it will remind me to keep my promise. And when you see a rainbow, think of my promise and be certain that I will keep it."

Abraham

GENESIS 12-13, 15, 18, 21

Abraham was one of Noah's descendants. He was a wealthy man and lived with his wife, Sarah, in a place called Haran. Although Abraham and Sarah had a happy life together, their one great sadness was that they had no children.

One day, God spoke to Abraham.
"I want you to take everything you own and go and live in the land of Canaan. There, I will make you the father of a great nation."
Abraham loved God, so he did as God asked. He gathered together all his sheep and goats, and made the long journey to Canaan with Sarah. His nephew Lot, and Lot's wife, also went with them.

At first, there was plenty of grass and water for Abraham's animals but, as the years passed and his flock grew bigger, there wasn't enough to feed them all.
"Let me go and live further down the valley," said Lot. "There will be much more grass and water down there."
Abraham would miss Lot, but knew it was the right thing to do.

Some years later, Abraham saw three men passing by close to his tent.
He invited them in to share a meal with him. When they had finished
eating, one of the men told Abraham that he had a message for him,
from God.
"You and Sarah are going to have a baby," the man smiled.
"But Sarah is far too old to have a baby!" Abraham exclaimed.

To his amazement, some months later Sarah gave birth to a baby boy.
They called him Isaac. It was then that Abraham remembered God's
words from many years ago: "I will make you the father of
a great nation."

Abraham was very proud that his son Isaac would be the first child of
that nation.

Moses in the Bulrushes

EXODUS 1-2

Many years after Joseph, Isaac's son, died, a new King came to power in Egypt. He hated the Hebrews and made them work as slaves, doing all the dirtiest and hardest jobs that the Egyptians didn't want to do. The King made them work very long hours and they were whipped and beaten if they tried to rest.

As there were more and more Hebrews being born in Egypt every year, the King became afraid that they would one day turn against their Egyptian masters and take over the whole country. So he ordered his soldiers to kill every Hebrew boy as soon as he was born. One clever Hebrew mother managed to hide her baby until he was three months old. After that, he was getting too big to hide, so she had to think of another way to protect him. His mother had named him Moses.

She took him down to the water's edge of the great River Nile and set him afloat in a small basket made of reeds. She was sad to see him float away, but knew it was the only way to save him. Her daughter, Miriam, followed the little basket as it floated away.

Some distance down the river, an Egyptian Princess was bathing in its clear waters. She noticed the basket as it bobbed its way towards her. When she looked inside, she was surprised to see a small baby.

"This must be a poor Hebrew child," she said to one of her handmaidens. The Princess felt so sorry for the little baby she decided to keep him.

Miriam, who had been hiding in the bulrushes, had an idea. She boldly approached the Princess.
"Your Highness," she said. "I know of a very caring Hebrew woman who could nurse this baby for you."

"Bring her to me!" ordered the Princess. Miriam ran off and returned with her mother who was secretly delighted to see her baby son again. She agreed that she would nurse Moses until he was older, then he would be taken to live with the Princess at the Palace.

A few years later, Moses went and lived with the Princess and she cared for him as if he was her own son.

From that day on, Moses was treated as an Egyptian Prince. When he became a young man it made him angry to see his people treated as slaves and he wondered how long he could keep his anger hidden. He never forgot that, deep down inside, he was still a Hebrew.

The Plagues of Egypt

EXODUS 7-12

Moses returned to Egypt and asked the King to set all the Hebrews free. But the King refused. An unhappy Moses asked for God's help. In order to change the King's mind, God promised he would cause strange and terrible things to happen in Egypt:

First the river turned red so no one could drink the water.

Then frogs came from the river and invaded the Egyptian houses.

Then swarms of terrible flies did the same.
Moses asked the King again if he would free the slaves.
Once again, the King refused.

Then all the animals began to die,

and terrible sores broke out all over the Egyptians' bodies.
But the King still would not set the Hebrews free.

Then violent storms ruined the crops,

and armies of locusts ate the few crops that were left.
But the King still would not free the slaves.

However, God told Moses that if the Hebrews killed a lamb and put a little of its blood on the door frames, then roasted and ate the lamb with bread and herbs, death would pass over them.

From that day on, this feast was known as the Passover. It celebrates the time when death passed over the Hebrew houses in Egypt.

The Parting of the Red Sea

EXODUS 14

After the deaths of the Egyptian children, the King had no choice but to let the slaves go free.

Moses gathered all the Hebrews together and led them out of Egypt. But the King became angry and ordered his soldiers to follow and kill every one of them.

When Moses heard the soldiers behind him, he realized there was no escape. The Red Sea lay straight ahead of them. Moses lifted his staff and commanded the sea to part, allowing the Hebrews to walk safely across.

When the last Hebrew reached the other side, the sea rushed back, drowning all the Egyptian soldiers who were following.

Moses in the Desert

EXODUS 15-17

After many weeks of walking through the barren desert, the Hebrews were tired and hungry.
"We were better off in Egypt," they said. "At least we had food and water there."

Moses was very worried but God spoke to him and comforted him. "Tell the people I will give them meat every evening and bread every morning, except on the seventh day, which will be My day of rest. That day will be called the Sabbath."

That evening, a huge flock of birds surrounded the tents where they slept. There were so many birds, they were easy to catch. At supper, the Hebrews filled their empty stomachs with the meat of the birds.

The next morning, the people looked out of their tents and saw that the ground was covered in seeds. The people gathered up as much of the seed as they could, ground it into flour and made it into bread.

"God has sent you this bread," Moses explained. "It is called Manna."

But soon the people were complaining again.
"We have no water to drink!" they grumbled. "How can we live without water?"
Moses turned to God for help, saying to him, "These people are dying of thirst and I have no water for them."
"Take your staff and strike the first rock you see," commanded God.
Moses followed God's command. He walked up to the first rock he saw and struck it with his staff. As soon as he did so, an enormous fountain of fresh water gushed out. Now that they had water as well as food, the people were happy at last.

God's Ten Laws

EXODUS 19-20

God told Moses to lead his people to the foot of Mount Sinai where something important would happen. They arrived at the foot of the mountain three months after they had left Egypt.

Moses asked the people to make camp and to wait for him.
Then he slowly started to climb to the top of Mount Sinai where
he knew God wanted to speak to him alone.
Moses was gone for many days. At the foot of the mountain, the Hebrew
people were getting restless.
"God has left us," they said to each other. "We must build
ourselves a new god to worship." So they collected all the gold in the
camp, melted it down and made a golden calf to which they began to
pray.

Moses came down from the mountain carrying two stone tablets that had the laws of God written on them. But when he saw the people worshiping the golden calf, he became angry and smashed the golden calf into little pieces.

"These are the laws of the only true God!" he said, pointing to the stone tablets. "Study them well and abide by them."

These were God's ten laws:

I am your one and true God. You must have no gods other than me.

You must not make false idols and worship them.

Always say My name with respect.

You must work for six days and rest on the seventh.

Always treat your mother and father with respect.

Do not kill any other human being.

People who are married must always be faithful to each other.

Do not steal.

It is wrong to tell lies.

Do not be envious of what other people have.

Ruth

RUTH 1-4

There was once a woman called Naomi who lived with her husband and two sons in Bethlehem. When famine struck, Naomi and her family went to live in a far off country called Moab. Her sons married girls called Orpah and Ruth.

Over the next ten years, Naomi's husband, and both sons died. Now an old woman, Naomi decided to make the long journey back to Bethlehem. Orpah and Ruth wanted to go with her, but Naomi begged them to stay and find new husbands in the country they knew.

Orpah agreed, but brave Ruth decided to take care of Naomi and to follow her wherever she went.

When they reached Bethlehem the harvest was beginning. Having little food, Ruth went into the fields every day hoping to pick up the ears of corn that had been missed. The farmer who owned the fields was a man called Boaz. He had heard how good Ruth had been to Naomi, and offered her all the water and corn she needed.

When Ruth told Naomi of Boaz's kindness, Naomi said, "This shows that God still cares for us. Even though our loved ones are dead, He has sent Boaz to help us."

Boaz started to care for Ruth, and asked her to marry him. Ruth happily agreed. Soon after, she gave birth to a baby boy. Naomi loved the boy very much and thanked God for giving her such a beautiful grandson.

David and Goliath

1 SAMUEL 16-17

Ruth's great grandson, David, worked on his father's farm. His job was to look after the sheep that grazed on the hills. He was a fearless boy who often had to defend his sheep against wild animals such as wolves and bears. He became an expert with a slingshot, which he fired stones with, to drive the wild animals away.

For years, King Saul of the Israelites had been fighting the Philistines. Down in the valley below David, a huge battle was about to take place. On one side of the valley lay the Israelite soldiers and, on the other, the mighty Philistine army.

One day, David's father asked him to take some food to his brothers who were soldiers in the Israelite army. As David got nearer, he could see the two great armies lined up opposite each other.

Suddenly, a giant of a man stepped out from the line of Philistine soldiers.

"My name is Goliath," he shouted to the Israelites. "I am the fiercest fighter in the world! No one can beat me! I challenge one of you to fight me! If you win, you win the battle for your whole army!"

The Israelite soldiers shrank back in fear. None of them dared to fight Goliath alone. Then David stepped forward.

"I'll fight you," he said. "I'm not afraid of you."

Goliath threw his head back and roared with laughter.

"Don't be silly, little boy. I will kill you in an instant."

"No, you won't," replied David. "I have God on my side."

King Saul tried to persuade David not to fight, but David's reply was simple and brave, "Do not worry, my King. God will help me."

Saul gave David his armour, but it was far too heavy for him to wear.

"I just need my slingshot and my faith in God," said David.
Then the giant and the boy walked out to fight each other. David bent down and picked up five smooth stones from the river bed.
All of a sudden, Goliath charged at him with a huge roar. David carefully loaded his slingshot with one of the stones, took aim and fired it at the giant. The stone hit Goliath right between the eyes, and buried deep in his forehead. He was stopped in an instant and fell dead at David's feet.

The Philistines could not believe that their hero, Goliath, was dead. The Israelites cheered their new hero, David, and chased the Philistine soldiers all the way back to their city gates. David was his country's saviour. He became famous throughout the land and eventually, when he grew up, became King of Israel.

King David

2 SAMUEL 5-11

Many years later, when David did become King of Israel, he had many other battles to fight; he fought against people who still supported the old King, Saul, and against the Philistines who longed to return to Israel.

David had always wanted to capture Jerusalem. In time, he succeeded, and made it God's city.

David was a much-loved King, but he had weaknesses that made God sad. Once, he fell in love with a woman called Bathsheba, but she was already married to a soldier in David's army. David wanted Bathsheba so much he arranged to have her husband killed.

Afterwards, he felt so guilty he spent many days praying for God's forgiveness.

God did forgive him and promised David he would remain as King, but David was disappointed when God gave the task of building a new Temple to David's son, Solomon, instead of him.

Later, David married Bathsheba. He remained a strong leader but it was a time of many problems for Israel.

Absalom

2 SAMUEL 14-18

Of all David's children, his son, Absalom, was the most loved. He was a handsome young man with thick, dark hair. He was also very proud and, because people loved him, he began to believe that he should be King.

Absalom asked his father, King David, to allow him to go to Hebron where he could worship God. But, when he got to Hebron, Absalom decided he was going to fight his father for the crown and raised a huge army.

King David was distraught when he heard of his son's plans, and sent out thousands of his own soldiers to meet Absalom's army.

There was a huge battle. David still loved his son, and told his army to show mercy to Absalom should they catch him. When Absalom's long hair became tangled in the branches of a tree, one of David's generals, Joab, disobeyed David's command and ordered three spears to be plunged into Absalom's chest, killing him immediately.

When David heard of his son's death, he wept. "I wish I had died instead of you," he cried. "Oh Absalom, my son, my son!"

King Solomon

1 KINGS 1-3

When King David became very old and weak, he took to ruling Israel from his bed. He knew that death was near, and wanted to be sure that the throne would pass into a safe pair of hands.

Years before, he had promised God that his son, Solomon, would be the new King when he died. But another of David's sons, Adonijah, grew ambitious and wanted the throne for himself.

When eventually Solomon did become King, Adonijah was afraid that Solomon might punish him for wanting the crown for himself. But Solomon told Adonijah that he would not harm him as long as he remained a good man.

Most of all, Solomon wanted to be wise. When God appeared to him in a dream, Solomon asked Him for the gift of wisdom. God promised He would make Solomon wise and, because Solomon asked for nothing but wisdom, God also promised him great wealth and a long life.

One day, two women came to see King Solomon. They had a baby with them, and each woman said that the baby belonged to her. They wanted Solomon to decide who was the real mother. "Bring me a sword," said Solomon. "I will cut the baby in half. In this way, you can share this child,"

One of the women agreed to this at once, but the other cried out, "No! I would rather see my baby brought up by another woman than see my child killed."

Solomon now knew for sure that this woman was the baby's true mother. Only the real mother would allow the child to be brought up by someone else rather than see it die.

"Take your baby," he said, handing the infant to the woman, "and go in peace."

God had been true to His word. He had made Solomon a great leader, and all the people of Israel marvelled at his wisdom.

The Dividing of Israel

1 KINGS 11

Solomon built many great cities and beautiful buildings while he was King. But all this had to be paid for, so there were many taxes that everyone had to pay. Also, more people were made to work directly for Solomon, rather than on their own land.

Over the years Solomon married many foreign princesses. But these princesses worshiped their own gods. After some time, Solomon began to worship these other gods, too.

"You have not been faithful to me," God told Solomon. "As a punishment, the kingdom of Israel will be taken from your son and divided up."

After Solomon's death, Israel was split in two. Solomon's son, Rehoboam, ruled Judah, in the south of the country, while King Jeroboam ruled the north.

Elijah

1 KINGS 17

After Jeroboam died none of the Kings who followed him were faithful to God. One of them, King Ahab, married a woman called Jezebel. She worshiped a god called Baal, and had many people killed who were loyal to God.

One day, a prophet called Elijah told King Ahab that God had warned him that it would not rain for years, and that many people would starve. Ahab was very angry with Elijah, but God told him to go to the Kerith valley where he would be safe.

Every day, God sent ravens to feed Elijah, and he drank water from a stream. But soon, because there was no rain, the stream dried up. Then God told Elijah to journey to Sidon where a woman would feed him.

When he saw a woman collecting a few sticks to make a fire, Elijah asked her for some food and water. The woman told him that she had only a little flour and a tiny drop of oil left. She was going to make one last loaf of bread for herself and her son before they starved to death. "Make two small loaves," Elijah told her, "and give one to me. From now on, you will find your flour and oil will never run out."

The woman did as Elijah asked and made him the loaf. Each day afterwards, she found there was just enough flour and oil left to make a loaf of bread with. She and her son never went hungry again.

One day, the woman's son became suddenly ill and died shortly after. The woman was heartbroken.

"Give your son's body to me," Elijah told her. He carried the body to the boy's bed and laid him on it. He then prayed to God three times, "Please, Lord, give this boy his life back."

Suddenly, the boy sat up, alive and well. God had heard Elijah's prayer and answered it. The boy's mother was overcome with joy and fell at Elijah's feet, saying, "You truly are a prophet of God."

The One True God

1 KINGS 18

It still hadn't rained in Israel for many years.
God told Elijah to go back to King Ahab.
"What do you want?" the King asked him angrily.
"Send the prophets and priests of your god, Baal, to
meet me at the top of Mount Carmel."
"And why should I do that?" asked Ahab.
"I want to prove that my God is the one true God," said
Elijah.

Ahab agreed to Elijah's test and, on a hot, dry day, sent
his priests and prophets on the long climb to the top of
Mount Carmel.
Elijah was waiting for them when they arrived.
He told them to build an altar with rocks and then to
place a dead bull on top of it.
"Now," said Elijah. "Offer this bull up to your god. Ask
him to send fire down from the sky and set light to it."
The priests and prophets called out to Baal for many
hours but nothing happened.

Elijah built his altar and placed a dead bull on it.
He then soaked the animal in water and stood back and prayed to
God to send fire. Even though the bull was wet through, it burst
into flames.

"Elijah's God is the true God!" everyone cried.

Then Elijah prayed for rain. For the first time in years, the sky
grew dark and rain began to fall in Israel.
When King Ahab and his wife, Jezebel, heard what Elijah had
done, they vowed to have him killed.
Elijah fled for his life and, after a long and tiring journey, found
himself at the foot of Mount Sinai.

"I am so lonely, Lord," he said to God. "I am your only prophet
left in Israel. All the others have been killed. Now the King and
Jezebel want to kill me, too."
"I know it is dangerous and you are frightened. But you must
return," said God. "There is much work to do there."

The King Will Come

MICAH 5

There were many times that God's people disobeyed Him. Sometimes they lost their faith that He was the only true God, and were tempted to worship other gods. But the prophets knew God only wanted peace for His people and that He had great plans for their future.

They knew that one day, a new King of Israel would be born in the little town of Bethlehem. He would be God's own son and he would spread God's laws throughout the whole world.

This new King would be called Jesus, and his story is told in the New Testament.

THE NEW TESTAMENT

Mary's Message

LUKE 1

Many years ago there lived a young girl called Mary. She was born in a village called Nazareth which was tucked away in the hills of Galilee.

Mary was very happy. She was engaged to be married to a carpenter called Joseph who also lived in the village.

One evening, as Mary sat quietly in her room, a blinding light suddenly appeared. She put her hand up to her face to shield her eyes but, through her fingers, Mary could make out a shimmering figure in the very centre of the light.

"Don't be afraid, Mary," said the figure. "I am Gabriel, an angel of God. I have come to give you a message."
The angel's voice was so beautiful that Mary lost all her fear.
"What message do you have for me?" she asked, calmly.
"I have come to tell you that you are going to have a baby," replied Gabriel.

"But I'm not even married yet," said Mary.
"The Holy Spirit will come down and God's power will rest upon you,"
said Gabriel. "You will have a baby and you must call him Jesus. And he
will be the Son of God."
"I am God's servant," Mary said quietly. "God's wish is my desire."
She raised her head, only to find herself in an empty room.
The angel Gabriel had left as silently as he had come.

Joseph the Carpenter

MATTHEW 1

Joseph the carpenter was an honest man. On hearing that his bride-to-be, Mary, was expecting a baby, he became very sad. "I am not the father of this child," he thought. "Therefore, I cannot marry her."

Being a good, caring man he decided to break off his engagement to Mary in private, so few people would know of her shame.

But one night he had a strange dream. In his dream, an angel of God appeared and said to him, "Do not break with Mary. She has done nothing wrong. The child she is carrying is the Son of God. You will name the baby Jesus. He will grow up to save the world from its sins."

When Joseph woke up, he thought about the dream. He realized that his dream was not a dream at all. It was a message from God. With a happy heart he began to make preparations to marry Mary as soon as possible.

The Birth of Jesus

LUKE 2

Mary and Joseph were married. They loved each other very much and were looking forward to the birth of their baby.

The happy couple started to prepare their home in Nazareth for the birth. Then they heard some news that would change everything: The Roman Emperor, Augustus, who ruled the land, had made a new law. The new law said that everyone who was not living in their place of birth had to return there to register for a new tax. Joseph was born in Bethlehem, so he and Mary had to go there straight away.

Joseph and Mary hurried, because the baby was due to be born very soon. They quickly gathered together some clothes, a few warm blankets and some food and water for the journey. They packed it all on their donkey and started out on the road to Bethlehem.

It was nightfall by the time they arrived, tired and hungry. Even worse, all the inns where they could have stayed were full. After searching for some hours, the only place where they could find shelter was an empty stable.

Joseph made the stable as comfortable as he could for his wife, who laid down to rest. Some time later, Mary gave birth to a little baby boy. She gave thanks for his safe delivery and called him Jesus, as the angel Gabriel had asked her to.

89

Three Wise Men

MATTHEW 2

One night, in a country far from Bethlehem, three wise men were riding their camels along a dusty road when they noticed a new star in the sky. It seemed to shine brighter than all the rest. "This star is a sign," they said. "It means a new King has been born. We must follow the star and it will lead us to him."

The star led them to the city of Jerusalem where King Herod ruled. Herod had already heard of the birth of a special baby in Bethlehem. He had learned from his priests that the baby would grow up to be the King of the Jews. Herod was angry and jealous. He didn't want to lose his power, especially to a baby born in a lowly stable.

He asked to meet the three wise men.
"I hear you are going to Bethlehem to worship a baby who will grow up to be King," he said. "Please tell me exactly where you find him, so I may go and worship him too."
The three wise men agreed, and the next morning they set out on the road to Bethlehem.

That night they arrived at the stable. When they saw the baby Jesus, they knelt down in front of him and offered him gifts. They had brought gold, sweet frankincense and myrrh. After they had blessed the child, the three wise men went quietly away and camped in the hills outside Bethlehem.

The wise men had planned to go back to Jerusalem the next morning and tell King Herod where to find the baby Jesus.

But that night they had a dream. In the dream, an angel advised them that if they told Herod where to find the baby boy, Herod would kill him. As dawn broke, they quickly packed their belongings on to their camels, and took a different road back to their own country. The road took them away from Herod.

At the same time, Joseph also had a dream. In it, an angel told him that the baby Jesus was in great danger. When he woke, Joseph told Mary of his dream. A worried Mary said they should leave at once. Joseph hurriedly loaded their donkey while Mary wrapped the sleeping Jesus in warm blankets. Then they started out on a long, long journey to a country called Egypt.

Joseph, Mary and Jesus lived in Egypt until King Herod died. Now that they were not in danger, they decided it was safe to return to Nazareth. At long last, they were going home.

The Boy Jesus

LUKE 2

Jesus was brought up in Nazareth and grew to be a strong and healthy boy. When he was twelve years old, Joseph and Mary decided he was old enough to travel to Jerusalem with them to celebrate the great feast of the Passover.

The journey took many days. When they arrived in Jerusalem, the streets were already full of people who had come from all over the country to celebrate Passover.

When the feast was over Mary and Joseph walked alongside the many people who were journeying back to Nazareth. Although they couldn't see Jesus, Mary and Joseph thought he must be with a group of children who were walking together.

When it became dark, everyone stopped to make camp. Joseph laid blankets on the ground, while Mary set out some food. But when they called for Jesus he didn't answer. They called again . . . there was still no reply. They searched all over the camp but Jesus was nowhere to be seen. They realized they must have left him behind in the city. A worried Joseph and Mary hurriedly packed their blankets and started back on the road to Jerusalem.

They searched for Jesus in Jerusalem for three days and nights.
Finally, they found him sitting in the Temple talking with the
teachers. They were amazed to see Jesus was not only listening
carefully to the teachers, but also asking questions that an ordinary
twelve year old would not think of.

"Where have you been?" asked Mary, relieved to see him again.
"We have been searching everywhere for you."
"I'm sorry I worried you," replied Jesus, calmly. "But I thought you
would know I'd be in my Father's house. I'll always be safe here."

Happy that he had come to no harm, Mary and Joseph forgave him, and
they all started the long journey back to Nazareth.

The First Miracle

JOHN 2

One day, Jesus was invited to a wedding. The marriage was to take place in Galilee, in a town called Cana. Jesus's mother, Mary, was invited too.

Everyone enjoyed themselves but, half way through the wedding feast, the wine ran out. "What are we to do?" asked the Master of the Feast. "How can we enjoy the rest of our food without wine?"

Mary overheard the worried man and thought Jesus might be able to do something about it. She whispered into her son's ear, "Can you help? This poor man has run out of wine to offer his guests."
"Do not ask me this," Jesus replied anxiously. "My time has not yet come."
But Mary was already turning to the servants, saying, "Do whatever he tells you to do."
Not wishing to disobey his mother, Jesus decided to help.

Nearby lay six empty water jars, from which the wedding guests had washed their hands before eating. Jesus told the servants to refill all six of the jars with water.

"Now," he said, "pour a little of the water into a cup and take it to the Master of the Feast."

The servants did as they were told.

When the Master of the Feast tasted the water, it had miraculously turned into wine.

"What wonderful wine! What a clever man you are!" he exclaimed, slapping the bridegroom on the back. "Everyone else serves the best wine first and keeps the cheapest until last. But you have saved the best until last!"

Only the servants who served the wine knew of Jesus's powers. This was the first miracle that Jesus ever performed.

Twelve Disciples

MARK 1, 3, LUKE 5, 6

Jesus was becoming famous throughout the land. Wherever he went, people flocked around to hear him speak of God. One day, he was speaking on the shores of the Sea of Galilee and, as usual, there was a large crowd pressing in on him so that they could hear every word.

Jesus was getting closer and closer to the water's edge. When he saw a fishing boat nearby, he asked the fishermen if they would take him a little way out to sea so the crowds could see him better. The fishermen were Andrew and his brother, Peter.

After he had finished speaking to the crowds, Jesus told Andrew and Peter to row out to deeper waters and cast their net.
"We've been fishing all night," they complained, "and we haven't even caught one fish!"
"Do as I tell you and you will be rewarded," Jesus replied.

The fishermen did as Jesus asked. When they hauled in their net, they were amazed to see it was so full of fish it was almost bursting! They called to their friends, James and John, who were fishing nearby, to help them take all the fish back to shore.

The fishermen were pleased with their catch but were frightened of Jesus's powers.

"Do not be scared," said Jesus, gently. "Come with me and I will make you fishers of men."

Andrew, Peter, James and John left their boats that day and followed Jesus wherever he went. They became his first disciples.

As Jesus journeyed through the country, preaching the word of God, he collected more disciples along the way. Soon there were twelve of them. Apart from the four fishermen of Galilee, there was Philip, Matthew, Thomas, Bartholomew, another James, Judas, Simon and Judas Iscariot. They all loved Jesus, and they, too, became messengers of God.

Jesus Heals the Sick

MATTHEW 8, LUKE 7, 18

As Jesus's fame grew and grew, more people flocked to his side, hoping to catch a glimpse of him. The ill and diseased fought their way through the crowds, hoping that Jesus would heal them.

One day a blind beggar, unable to push his way to Jesus's side, shouted out, "Son of David, have mercy on me!"
Jesus heard the blind man's call and asked that he be brought to him.
"What do you want from me?" Jesus asked.
"Lord, let me see!" pleaded the beggar.
Jesus laid his hands on the man's head, and said, "Receive your sight. Your faith has healed you."
When Jesus took his hands away, the beggar could see again.

Another time, Jesus was asked to visit the house of a Roman soldier. The soldier's servant was very ill and close to death.
As Jesus neared his house, the soldier rushed out to meet him.

"Lord, although I am not worthy to have you enter my home, please say a prayer so my servant will be healed."
Jesus was surprised and moved by the strength of the soldier's belief in him.
"I have not seen faith as strong as this in the whole of Israel," he said.

After Jesus had left him, the soldier went back into his house and found his servant completely cured of his illness.

The Good Shepherd

MATTHEW 18, LUKE 15, JOHN 10

Jesus often told people stories, so they could understand more easily what he was trying to teach them.

All sorts of people came to listen to Jesus. Some of them had done bad things in their lives. Many teachers of God's Word thought that Jesus should not be speaking with people who had done wrong. But Jesus thought that everyone should have the chance to be forgiven. He told this simple story to make them understand.

"If a shepherd has a hundred sheep," said Jesus, "and one sheep takes a wrong path and gets lost, what does the shepherd do? He makes sure the other ninety-nine sheep are safe and then looks for the one missing sheep. He does not stop looking until he finds it. Then the shepherd will ask his friends and family to celebrate with him the return of the lost sheep."

"It is the same for people," Jesus continued. "When they get lost and stray from the path to God, they sometimes do bad things.
But there is joy in Heaven when they find the path that leads them to God again."

"I am like that shepherd," said Jesus. "I help people who have strayed from the path to God, and I lead them to Him again. People are like my sheep. I will always protect them. I love them, and I would die for them."

Seeds that Fall

MATTHEW 13, MARK 4, LUKE 8

Jesus used to tell another story to make people understand God's message. It was about a man who sowed seed.

"One day a man went out with a bag of seed to sow," began Jesus. "Some of the seed he threw fell on a stony path, where birds flew down and ate it."

"Some of the seed fell on rough, rocky ground where there was hardly any soil. When the corn began to sprout into young plants, the strong sun dried them up and they died."

"Some of the seed fell among weeds. As the young corn plants tried to grow, the weeds wrapped themselves around the plants and choked them."

"But some seed fell on good ground. The young plants grew well and produced much corn."
Jesus then explained this story to his followers.

115

"Some people are like the seed which fell on the stony path: they hear God's message but choose not to believe it."

"Other people are like the seed that fell on the rough, stony ground: they, too, hear God's message but, when life becomes hard, they choose not to obey it."

"And some people are like the seed that fell amongst the weeds: they let their love of money and possessions blind them to God's message."

"But for people who are like the seed that fell on the good ground, they are blessed. They have heard God's message. They understand that God's Word is the truth, and they try every day to obey His laws."

Jairus's Daughter

MATTHEW 9, MARK 5, LUKE 8

There was once a man called Jairus who was the leader of a synagogue. One day, while Jesus was preaching, Jairus pushed his way through the crowds to see him.

"Help me, Master," he said. "My little daughter is very ill. I'm afraid she's going to die. Please come to my house and see her."

Jesus agreed at once. He and Jairus began to make their way through the throngs of people that now followed Jesus everywhere.

When a woman touched Jesus's robe as he passed by, Jesus turned and asked, "Who touched me?" The woman stepped forward.

"I did, Master. I have been ill for many years. Now that I have touched your robe, I am healed."

"Your faith has made you well," said Jesus. "Go in peace."

A messenger from Jairus's house was sent out to meet them.
"I have bad news for you, Jairus," he said. "Your daughter has died."
Jairus fell to the ground with grief.

At Jairus's house, many people were standing outside weeping.
Jesus comforted them.
"The girl is not dead. She is just sleeping," he said.
Jesus went to the girl's side and took her hand.
"Get up, my child," he said, softly.
The girl slowly opened her eyes and then climbed out of bed as Jesus
had commanded. She was completely cured.

Feeding the Five Thousand

MATTHEW 14, MARK 6, LUKE 9, JOHN 6

One day, Jesus was speaking on a hillside near to the shores of Lake Galilee. Over five thousand people had come to hear his words. By the evening everyone was still there, listening intently to what he had to say.

One of his disciples rushed up to him.
"Lord, these people have been here all day with nothing to eat. They must be very hungry, and all I can find is a small boy who has five loaves of bread and two fishes."
"Bring him to me," said Jesus.
When the boy arrived, Jesus took the basket of loaves and fishes from him and bowed his head in prayer.
Jesus then began to walk among the people, handing out the food.

Amazingly, the small basket of loaves and fishes never seemed to run out. Eventually, all five thousand people had been fed until they could eat no more. There was even enough food left over to fill twelve large baskets.

The Good Samaritan

LUKE 10

"What does 'love thy neighbor' mean?" someone once asked Jesus.

"Listen," said Jesus, "and I will tell you."

Then Jesus told this story: "There was once a man who was on his way from Jerusalem to Jericho. On a lonely stretch of the road, some thieves set upon him. They hit him and kicked him many times, and took all his money."

"Later, a priest happened to pass by. He took one look at the man lying at the side of the road and, pretending not to see him, passed by without helping him."

"Not long after, another priest passed by. He, too, couldn't be bothered to help the poor man, and just kept on walking."

"A few hours later, another man passed by. This man was a Samaritan. Samaritans and Jews did not like one another. But this Samaritan was kind. He comforted the man, let him drink from his water bottle and bandaged his wounds. Then he helped him onto his donkey and took him to a nearby inn where the man could rest. 'Here's some money,' he said to the innkeeper. 'Please let this man stay until he is well. If I owe you any more, I will pay you next time I am passing through.'"

When Jesus finished his story, he said to everyone listening, "The Samaritans and the Jews hated each other, yet it was a Samaritan who helped the Jew when he most needed it. This is what I mean when I tell you to 'love thy neighbor'."

"No matter how different a person may be from you, we are all God's children, and we should be kind to everyone."

The Paralyzed Man

MATTHEW 9, MARK 2, LUKE 5

Once, Jesus was teaching inside someone's house. As usual, there were hundreds of people who wanted to get close to him and hear what he was saying. The house quickly filled up with many people, and there were lots more outside, crowding around the door and windows hoping to get a glimpse of him.

Suddenly, four men approached the house. They were carrying their friend on a bed mat. He had suffered a terrible disease that had left him paralyzed. His friends were taking him to see Jesus, whom they hoped would help. But, there were so many people crowding around the door, it was impossible to get through.

One of the men had an idea. "Why don't we cut a hole in the roof," he said. "It's only made of straw. Then we can lower our friend into the room where Jesus is."

The others agreed and, soon, the paralyzed man was lying at Jesus's feet.

When Jesus saw what the men had done, he was moved by the care they had shown their friend.

He knelt down by the paralyzed man and took his hand. "Your sins are forgiven. Now stand, pick up your mat and go home."
The man did as Jesus told him. He was completely cured, and everyone who saw the miracle was amazed.

Entering Jerusalem

MATTHEW 21, MARK 11, LUKE 19, JOHN 12

Although Jesus knew his time on Earth was coming to an end, he and his disciples decided to go to Jerusalem to celebrate the feast of the Passover. Jesus rode on the back of a donkey as he entered the city. People lined the road to see him. It was as if a king had come. They threw their shawls down in front of him and cut down palm leaves to lay in his path.

When Jesus arrived at the Temple he became very angry. Instead of people praying, the Temple was full of people making money by buying and selling things.

Jesus was so upset, he overturned their tables and drove everyone out, shouting after them: "This house should be a house of prayer, but you have turned it into a den of thieves!"
The Temple leaders were shocked by Jesus's behaviour. They feared that Jesus was becoming too powerful. They wanted to get rid of him. Soon, they would have their chance.

The Betrayal of Jesus

MATTHEW 26, MARK 14, LUKE 22

One of Jesus's disciples was called Judas Iscariot. Judas had started to believe that Jesus was not who he said he was, that he was not the true Son of God. These thoughts made Judas do something terrible.

One afternoon, while the rest of the disciples were buying food in the market for the feast of the Passover, Judas secretly sneaked away to meet the Temple priests. He knew that the priests were not pleased with Jesus and wanted to be rid of him.

"I am with Jesus all the time," he whispered to them. "I can tell you where you can arrest him quietly, away from the crowds."
"How much do you want for this information?" the priests asked him.
"Thirty pieces of silver," replied Judas.
The Temple priests gave him the money and, when he'd left, smiled contentedly together.
"Soon, Jesus will be ours!" they said.

"My time in this world has almost come to an end," he continued.
"Tonight, one of you will betray me."
The disciples became angry when they heard this.
"Who, Lord? Which one of us could do such a thing?" they cried.
"The one I pass this bread to," said Jesus.
He broke off some bread and passed it to Judas, saying to him,
"Go, do what you have to do."
Judas stood up, hung his head in shame and left the room, walking quickly into the dark night.

After Judas had left, Jesus broke up the rest of the bread and passed it to each of the disciples.

"Eat this bread which is my body, and remember me," he told them. Then he lifted up a cup of wine.

"Drink this wine which is my blood," he said, "and remember me." Everyone was sad. They prayed and sang a hymn together, before leaving the room.

The Garden of Gethsemane

MATTHEW 26, MARK 14, LUKE 22, JOHN 18

Jesus and his disciples walked up the Mount of Olives and into the Garden of Gethsemane.

On the way, Jesus told Peter that Peter would deny knowing him three times later that night.

"I would never say I didn't know you," said Peter. "I love you, Lord. I would rather die than pretend I didn't know you."

"We shall see," replied Jesus.

Jesus asked Peter, James and John to enter the garden with him. The rest of the disciples kept guard near the garden's gates. He left Peter, James and John after a while and walked further into the garden by himself so he could be alone to pray.

"I am scared, Father," he prayed to God. "I do not wish to die, but if it is Your will, then so be it."

When he returned, he found that Peter, James and John had fallen asleep.

"Could you not stay awake for even one hour?" he asked them, and then left them to pray again.

When he returned, they had fallen asleep again. This happened for a third time, after which, the disciples were woken up by shouting at the gates, and by torches that lit up the sky.

It was the priests from the Temple with the Temple guards. They were being led by Judas, and had come to take Jesus away. Judas walked straight up to Jesus and kissed him.

"This is he," said Judas, turning to the soldiers, who grabbed Jesus roughly by the arms. Peter was so angry at the way they were treating Jesus, he drew his sword and cut an ear off one of the priest's guards.

"Put your sword away, Peter," said Jesus, quietly. He touched the guard's ear and made it whole again.

Then the soldiers led Jesus out of the garden. The disciples were so frightened, they ran away.

Later that night, Peter was asked three times if he was a friend of Jesus. Peter denied knowing him each time he was asked. When he realized what he had said, he leaned against a tree and wept.

Jesus on Trial

MATTHEW 27, MARK 15, LUKE 23, JOHN 18-19

The priests of the Temple had decided that Jesus must die, but they were not allowed to put anyone to death. So they had Jesus dragged in front of the Roman governor, Pontius Pilate.
He was a powerful man who had the authority to order an execution.

"What has he done wrong?" Pontius Pilate asked the priests.
"He says he is a king," they replied.
"Are you the King of the Jews?" Pontius Pilate asked Jesus.
"You say I am," said Jesus and, bowing his head, refused to answer any more questions.

Pontius Pilate thought Jesus was innocent and asked the crowd,
"This man has done nothing wrong. What would you have me do with him?" "Crucify him!" the crowd yelled back.

Under Roman law, Pontius Pilate had the power to set one prisoner free during Passover.

"Whom shall I set free?" he asked the crowd. "This man Jesus or this common murderer, Barabbas?"

"Set Barabbas free," they shouted. "Crucify Jesus!"

"Very well," he said. "You shall have your way. Barabbas will be set free, but Jesus will be crucified!"

Carrying the Cross

MATTHEW 27, MARK 15, LUKE 23, JOHN 18-19

Jesus was handed over to some Roman soldiers who beat and whipped him until he was very weak. As he lay on the ground bleeding, the soldiers began to laugh at him and mock him.

"Oh, Your Majesty," said one of them. "I've made a special crown for you."

And he put a crown made of thorns on Jesus's head.

"Here's your royal robe," jeered another soldier, putting an old purple shawl around Jesus's shoulders.

Then it was time for Jesus to carry the cross, on which he would be nailed, to the place of crucifixions. He stumbled through the streets bearing the heavy, wooden cross on his back. Behind him, the Roman soldiers were taunting him and whipping him on.

After a while, Jesus did not have the strength to stand. So the soldiers told a man they saw in the crowd to help Jesus carry the cross. This man's name was Simon.

Finally, they reached the place where Jesus was to be crucified.
It lay just outside the city and was called Golgotha.

The Crucifixion

MATTHEW 27, MARK 15, LUKE 23, JOHN 18-19

The soldiers ripped Jesus's clothes from him and laid him on the cross while it was still on the ground. They nailed his hands and feet to the cross, and put a sign on it which said: 'Jesus of Nazareth. King of The Jews'. Then they raised the cross, and set it in the ground between two thieves, who were also being crucified.

People in the crowd jeered at Jesus.
"Save yourself if you are truly the Son of God," they shouted.
But Jesus said nothing. His mother, Mary, was standing with John, one of Jesus's disciples. She wept at her son's suffering.
"Look after my mother as if you were her own son," said Jesus looking down at John.

At midday, the sky suddenly went dark and stayed that way for three hours. Jesus cried out, "My God! My God! Why have you forsaken me?"

A little while later, he asked for some water to help his thirst. A cruel soldier gave him a sponge, soaked in vinegar, to drink from.

Shortly after, Jesus gave a terrible cry, and whispered, "It is finished." Then he closed his eyes and died. At that moment, the ground shook and the curtain in the Temple ripped from top to bottom.
One Roman soldier looked up wide-eyed with wonder at Jesus's body on the cross.
"Truly," he said. "This man was the Son of God."

The Empty Tomb

MATTHEW 27-28, MARK 15-16, LUKE 23-24, JOHN 19-20

After Jesus's body was taken down from the cross, it was wrapped in a sheet and taken to a cave which would serve as Jesus's tomb. A large rock was laid across its entrance.

Three days later, Mary Magdalene went with a friend to pray outside the tomb. To the women's amazement, they found that the rock had been rolled away from the entrance. When they looked inside, they saw that Jesus's body was gone. All that was left inside was the sheet that he had been wrapped in.

Two of the disciples, Peter and John, were sent for. They too were puzzled as to what had happened. John became scared and didn't want to go into the tomb. Peter thought the body might have been stolen, but secretly hoped that Jesus had risen from the dead.

Later, when everyone had left, Mary Magdalene stayed by the tomb and began to pray. She was so puzzled and upset, she started to cry. "Where is my Lord?" she wept. "Where have they taken him?" Then, she felt a comforting hand on her shoulder and a voice asked her quietly, "Why do you weep so?"

"Because they have taken my Lord away," she replied.

"Mary, do you not know me?" said the voice, softly. "It is I."

Mary turned around and was astonished to see Jesus standing by her side.

"Do not be afraid," Jesus said. "For soon, I will be with my Father in Heaven. Go now, and tell the others that you have seen me."

Full of joy, Mary rushed to tell the disciples that she had seen Jesus and spoken with him.

Jesus and Peter

JOHN 21

Shortly after Jesus had risen from the tomb, Peter was out fishing on the Sea of Galilee. He and some other disciples had been fishing all night, but had not caught a single fish.

All of a sudden a man shouted at them from the shore, "Throw your net over the right side of the boat."
Nobody recognized that the man was Jesus. They did as they were told, and when they pulled up the net, it was full of fish.

"Only Jesus could have done this," said one of the disciples.

Peter was so excited to see Jesus again he swam to the shore to greet him. By the time the others caught up, Jesus had already lit a fire.

"Let us cook some of the fish you caught," he said.

After eating, Jesus asked Peter if he loved him.

"You know I do," replied Peter.

Jesus asked him the question twice more. Each time Peter gave the same reply, "You know I do."

Jesus smiled and, hugging Peter, told him he should always care for the other disciples.

The Last Word

ACTS 1

The last time the disciples saw Jesus was on the Mount of Olives. He had come to say goodbye to them.

"You must speak bravely and honestly about me," said Jesus. "You must spread God's teachings to the furthest parts of this country, and to people from other countries, too. In this way the Word of God and His love will spread throughout the whole world."

Then a mist came down and covered Jesus so that the disciples could not see him anymore. When the mist cleared, Jesus had disappeared. He had been taken to Heaven to be with his Father, Almighty God, and to sit by His side forever.